# Black's Sketchbooks

London · Adam & Charles Black

PUBLISHED BY
A. & C. BLACK · SOHO SQUARE · LONDON W.

# The ENGLISH LAKES

## A Sketch Book
## by Gordon Home

Langdale Pikes
from a garden
on the banks
of Windermere

A & C Black Ltd. Soho Square · London W.

# Sketches

*Published Spring, 1922.*

Windermere
from Bowness

Dove Cottage
Wordsworth's home
at Grasmere

Stone-circle
near Keswick.—
Helvellyn in distance.

GORDON HOME

Derwentwater from near Friar's Crag.

Corner Spit House

Gorgon's
Head

Derwentwater & Skiddaw
from the South

Scale Force
The innermost recess.

Among the summit
of the fells.
Looking North from
the Pillar

Congost Home

Ennerdale Water.
Whitehaven & the Irish Sea beyond

Wasindier
the Jorego on left

Conyong Home

Clouds dispersing
on Scafell viewed
from Pillar Fell

A corner of Wastwater on right

Styhead Pass
looking west.
(Lingmell on left)

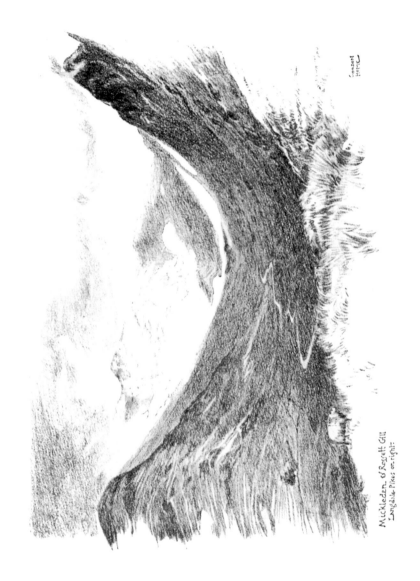

Mickleden, & Rossett Gill
Langdale Pikes on right.

Ullswater —
from the summit of
Helvellyn. Swirrel Edge & Red Tarn
in the foreground

Hawes Water
Harter Fell beyond

Gordon
Home

First published in Great Britain in 1922
by A&C Black Publishers
36 Soho Square
London W1D 3QY
www.acblack.com

This edition published 2009

© 1922, 2009 A&C Black

ISBN 978-1-408-11554-1

A CIP record of this book is available from the British Library

Printed and bound in China